Mel Bay's

DRUM ME~~THOD~~

By William Schinstine and Fred Hoey

This method was written to incorporate the latest ideas in teaching percussion to the student. The authors are proven writers in the field of percussion and have a wealth of experience in dealing with the problems of teaching modern drum technique.

Bill Bay

STUDENT PRACTICE TIPS

1. Look through your lesson and be sure you understand what you are to do.

2. Start your practicing by playing a review piece you know and enjoy playing. Use it as a sort of warm up.

3. Start new things slowly and count along as you play. Be sure you get the sticking correct and the rhythms accurate.

4. If you have difficulty, slow down until you can play it. Then gradually speed up the piece.

5. If you can't figure something out, ask for help. Call your teacher or an older student. Don't just give up.

6. Be concerned about your hand positions and movements. Check them frequently. Play in front of a mirror.

7. Be as concerned about how loudly or softly you play as you are about rhythmic accuracy.

8. Tape record yourself frequently to hear if you are satisfied with the results of your practice.

9. Always look ahead at what you might expect in your next lesson. Pay attention at each lesson so that you understand the new things.

10. Be sure you know when your next lesson time is to be. Try to get there a few minutes early so you are ready when it is your time.

1 2 3 4 5 6 7 8 9 0

TABLE OF CONTENTS

Page 3....Parts of the Snare Drum
Page 4....Holding your Drum Sticks
Page 5....Balance Point, Choosing the Correct Stick
Page 6....Striking the Drum and Tuning the Drum
Page 7....Exercise #1
Page 8....Review and Exercise #2
Page 9....Quarter Notes
Page 10...Bouncing Your Sticks
Page 11...Time Signatures
Page 12...Changing Time
Page 13...Whole and Half Notes and the Tie
Page 14...Duet and Quarter Note Bounce
Page 15...Student Test #1
Page 16...Exercise #11 and Exercise #12
Page 17...Exercise #13 and #14
Page 18...Introducing Eighth Notes
Page 19...Eighth Rests
Page 20...Bouncing on Eighth Notes
Page 21...6/8 Time
Page 22...Repeats and Endings
Page 23...Test Your Skills
Page 24...Dynamics and Use of a Metronome
Page 25...Review Piece
Page 26...Creative Writing #1
Page 27...16th Notes
Page 28...16th Note Rhythms, 2/4 Time
Page 29...Duets with 16th Notes
Page 30...Creative Writing #2
Page 31...Cut Time
Page 32...Cut Time Duet
Page 33...Bounces to Rolls
Page 34...Cut Time Rolls, Cut Off March
Page 35...Creative Writing #3
Page 36...Roll Duets
Page 37...Student Test #2
Page 38...Dotted Notes and Their Values
Page 39...6/8 With 16th Notes
Page 40...6/8 Duet
Page 41...6/8 Bounces to Rolls, Drum Solo
Page 42...Basic Stick Strokes
Page 43...Student Test #3
Page 44...Direct Follow Through Flams
Page 45...Reverse Follow Through Flams
Page 46...No Follow Through Flams
Page 47...Student Test #4
Page 48...Purple Flame Duet
Page 49...Final Playing Test
Page 50...Final Written Test
Page 51...Student Practice Tips
Page 52...Certificate of Completion

FIG. 1

SETTING UP THE SNARE DRUM

Figure 1 above shows the correct position of snare drum on stand with snare strainer near single arm of snare stand basket.

The snare drum on stand should have the proper playing angle. The drum should be parallel to the floor or tilted at a slight angle moving downward from the left hand to the right as shown in Fig. 1.

TEACHER'S MAKE SURE BOX

1. GET ACQUAINTED.
2. ACQUAINT STUDENTS WITH THEIR EQUIPMENT.
3. EXPLAIN HAND POSITIONS. MAKE SURE THAT THE STUDENT UNDERSTANDS THE HAND POSITIONS.
4. DEMONSTRATE HOW TO STRIKE THE DRUM.
5. INTRODUCE THE BASIC STICK EXERCISES AS A ROTE LESSON.

DELUXE DRUM KIT

SNARE DRUM PARTS & ACCESSORIES

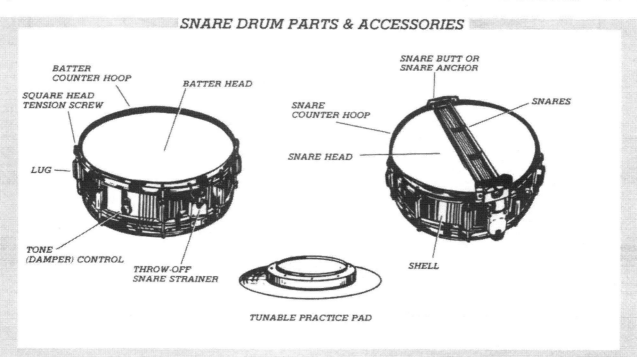

TUNABLE PRACTICE PAD

A CHOICE FOR HOLDING YOUR DRUM STICKS

The cause of most student difficulties can be traced to incorrect hand positions. The foundations of good drumming technique are correct hand positions. The following pictures illustrate the correct hand positions from various views. Study and refer to them often.

☆ THE MATCHED GRIP

The Matched Grip is the simplest way to hold drum sticks correctly. In the opinion of the authors, the Matched Grip should be recommended for the beginning percussionist. Each hand holds the stick exactly the same. With the Matched grip the stick becomes an extension of the arm.

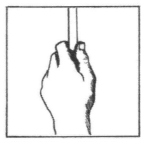

FIG. 2 View of the left hand

FIG. 3 View of the right hand

FIG. 4 View of the left hand from the right side

FIG. 5 The Right Hand as it would appear in a mirror

THE TRADITIONAL GRIP
THE LEFT HAND POSITION

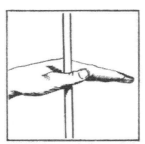

FIG. 6 Grasp the stick between the thumb & 1st finger

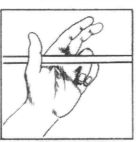

FIG. 7 Place the 3rd finger & pinky under the stick

FIG. 8 Place the 1st finger & ½ the 2nd finger over the stick

FIG. 9 View as seen in a mirror

THE RIGHT HAND POSITION

THE CONCERT GRIP   THE PARADE GRIP

FIG. 10 View from the left side

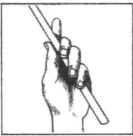

FIG. 11 Front view as it would appear in a mirror

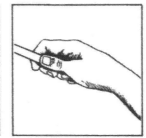

FIG. 12 View from the left side

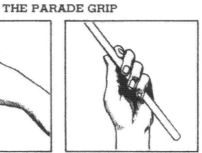

FIG. 13 Front view as it would appear in a mirror

A CHOICE OF DRUM STICKS

The models of SNARE DRUM STICKS listed below are suggested as the most practical choice for the beginning percussionist. These selections represent distinctive models and styles. Brand names are not listed.

5A	**16″**	SMALL SHAFT FOR SMALLEST HAND—MAXIMUM TAPER FOR BOUNCE AND FEEL.
5B	**16″**	SHAFT SLIGHTLY THICKER FOR MEDIUM HAND—THINNEST OF "B" MODEL STICKS WITH SAME BASIC TAPER OF 5A, YET SIZED SLIGHTLY THICKER THAN 5A.
2B	**16″**	THE "UNIVERSAL" MODEL—THE HEAVIEST STICK RECOMMENDED FOR BEGINNER'S. LARGER HEAD AND SHAFT THAN 5B.

THE BALANCE POINT

"Balance Point" in *matched grip* is the "fulcrum" where the thumb and forefinger of each hand meet on the stick indicated in **FIG. 14**. In *"traditional grip"* the balance point or "fulcrum" is the same as the right hand matched grip while the "V" formed by the thumb and forefinger of the left hand forms the balance point of the traditional left hand grip indicated in **FIG. 15**.

BEAD
OR
TIP

BUTT

BALANCE POINT

▰ THE BASIC RULE TO FIND THE BALANCE POINT ▰

Measure from the butt end of stick a distance equal to one third of the total length of the stick. Mark the Balance Point on each stick. **MEASURING THE BALANCE POINT IS A MUST BEFORE AND DURING EVERY PRACTICE SESSION.**

Regardless of grip, each stick must have 2/3rd″ of length available for equal "stroke" and "sound."

The "Balance Point" promotes an "even sound" by basically fostering an "even" or "like" 2/3rds of the stick for Basic Balance.

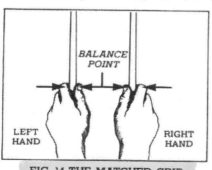

FIG. 14 THE MATCHED GRIP

CHECKING
THE
BALANCE
POINT

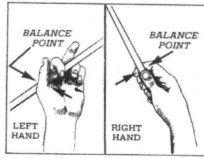

FIG. 15 THE TRADITIONAL GRIP

REMEMBER TO CHECK THE BALANCE POINT BEFORE & DURING EACH PRACTICE SESSION.

STICK POSITIONS
STRIKING THE DRUM

FIG. 16 Strike the drum near the Center for most playing

FIG. 17 Strike the drum near the Far Edge for a Softer sound

FIG. 18 View of the Matched Grip position with both sticks near the center

FIG. 19 View showing the Right Hand Down Stroke

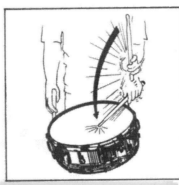

FIG. 20 View showing the Left Hand Down Stroke

On the following pages, you will find "guidesigns" indicating proper stroke and proper sticking.

 INDICATES DOWN STROKE WITH RIGHT HAND

 INDICATES DOWN STROKE WITH LEFT HAND

STROKE AND STICKING GUIDE

TUNING (TENSIONING) THE SNARE DRUM

FIG. 21 THE BATTER HEAD

USING THE DRUM KEY, TIGHTEN ONE TURN AT A TIME—ACROSS FROM EACH OTHER—EXAMPLE 1-2-3-4 ETC AS SHOWN IN FIG 21. THE BATTER HEAD SHOULD HAVE A MINIMUM OF FOUR FULL TURNS—MAXIMUM SIX. THE SNARE HEAD (FIG. 22) SHOULD BE TUNED IN THE SAME WAY WITH A MINIMUM OF FOUR TURNS AND A MAXIMUM OF SIX. TO CHECK EVEN TENSION ON EITHER HEAD COUNT THE THREADS ON THE TENSION SCREW. ALL SCREWS SHOULD HAVE THE SAME NUMBER SHOWING ABOVE THE LUG IF EVEN TENSION HAS BEEN APPLIED. TO ADJUST THE SNARES, USE ONE HALF TURNS OF THE SNARE TENSION KNOB. MAXIMUM TENSION SHOULD BE FOUR HALF TURNS.

FOR CRISP SOUNDS AND FOR FINE TUNING THE SNARE HEAD CAN BE TUNED SLIGHTLY TIGHTER THAN THE BATTER HEAD.

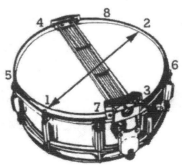

FIG. 22 SHOWING THE SNARE HEAD

EXERCISE NO. 1

"Daily Playing Exercise" starts with 10 down strokes (designated by ♀) with each hand progressing to one stroke with each hand. This process is reversed by starting with one stroke with each hand and progressing to 10. This exercise is to be read across the page from left to right.

READ ACROSS THE PAGE FROM LEFT TO RIGHT

LINE

A	RIGHT HAND →	①②③④⑤⑥⑦⑧⑨⑩
B	LEFT HAND →	①②③④⑤⑥⑦⑧⑨⑩
C	RIGHT HAND →	①②③④⑤⑥⑦⑧⑨
D	LEFT HAND →	①②③④⑤⑥⑦⑧⑨
E	RIGHT HAND →	①②③④⑤⑥⑦⑧
F	LEFT HAND →	①②③④⑤⑥⑦⑧
G	RIGHT HAND →	①②③④⑤⑥⑦
H	LEFT HAND →	①②③④⑤⑥⑦
I	RIGHT HAND →	①②③④⑤⑥
J	LEFT HAND →	①②③④⑤⑥
K	RIGHT HAND →	①②③④⑤
L	LEFT HAND →	①②③④⑤
M	RIGHT HAND →	①②③④
N	LEFT HAND →	①②③④
O	RIGHT HAND →	①②③
P	LEFT HAND →	①②③
Q	RIGHT HAND →	①②
R	LEFT HAND →	①②
S	RIGHT HAND →	①
T	LEFT HAND →	①

WHEN YOU HAVE FINISHED LINES A THRU T, START AT THE BOTTOM (LINE T) AND WORK BACK TO THE TOP THRU LINE A.

REPEAT THIS PAGE FIVE TIMES EACH DAY

1. MORNING 2. AFTER SCHOOL 3. BEFORE SUPPER 4. AFTER SUPPER 5. BEFORE BED

Hold your drum sticks in the proper positions every time you watch TV this week. Keep shifting them from hand to hand until you can remember the position.

REVIEW

1. REVIEW DAILY EXERCISE NO. 1 PAGE 7 FORWARD AND BACKWARD.

2. VARY DAILY EXERCISE SO IT READS AS FOLLOWS:

READ ACROSS THE PAGE FROM LEFT TO RIGHT

	RIGHT HAND	LEFT HAND	RIGHT HAND	LEFT HAND	RIGHT HAND	LEFT HAND	RIGHT HAND	LEFT HAND	RIGHT HAND	LEFT HAND	RIGHT HAND	LEFT HAND	RIGHT HAND	LEFT HAND	RIGHT HAND	LEFT HAND
NUMBER OF STROKES EACH HAND ►10	10	8	9	7	8	6	7	5	6	4	5	3	4	2	3	1
►1	1	3	2	4	3	5	4	6	5	7	6	8	7	9	8	10

EXERCISE NO. 2

STRIKE DRUM IN CENTER OF HEAD

Ⓛ = STRIKE LEFT HAND   Ⓡ = STRIKE RIGHT HAND

LINE 1. Ⓡ Ⓛ Ⓡ Ⓛ | Ⓡ Ⓛ Ⓡ Ⓛ | Ⓡ Ⓛ Ⓡ Ⓛ | Ⓡ

LINE 2. Ⓛ Ⓡ Ⓛ Ⓡ | Ⓛ Ⓡ Ⓛ Ⓡ | Ⓛ Ⓡ Ⓛ Ⓡ | Ⓛ

WATCH FOR STICKING CHANGES!

LINE 3. Ⓡ Ⓡ Ⓡ Ⓡ | Ⓛ Ⓛ Ⓛ Ⓛ | Ⓡ Ⓡ Ⓡ Ⓡ | Ⓛ

LINE 4. Ⓛ Ⓛ Ⓛ Ⓛ | Ⓡ Ⓡ Ⓡ Ⓡ | Ⓛ Ⓛ Ⓛ Ⓛ | Ⓡ

LINE 5. Ⓡ Ⓡ Ⓛ Ⓛ | Ⓡ Ⓡ Ⓛ Ⓛ | Ⓡ Ⓡ Ⓛ Ⓛ | Ⓡ

LINE 6. Ⓛ Ⓛ Ⓡ Ⓡ | Ⓛ Ⓛ Ⓡ Ⓡ | Ⓛ Ⓛ Ⓡ Ⓡ | Ⓛ

LINE 7. Ⓡ Ⓛ Ⓛ Ⓛ | Ⓡ Ⓛ Ⓛ Ⓛ | Ⓡ Ⓛ Ⓛ Ⓛ | Ⓡ

LINE 8. Ⓛ Ⓡ Ⓡ Ⓡ | Ⓛ Ⓡ Ⓡ Ⓡ | Ⓛ Ⓡ Ⓡ Ⓡ | Ⓛ

PRACTICE THREE TIMES DAILY: MORNING, AFTER SCHOOL, AFTER SUPPER.

EXERCISE NO. 3
LEARNING ABOUT QUARTER NOTES ♩

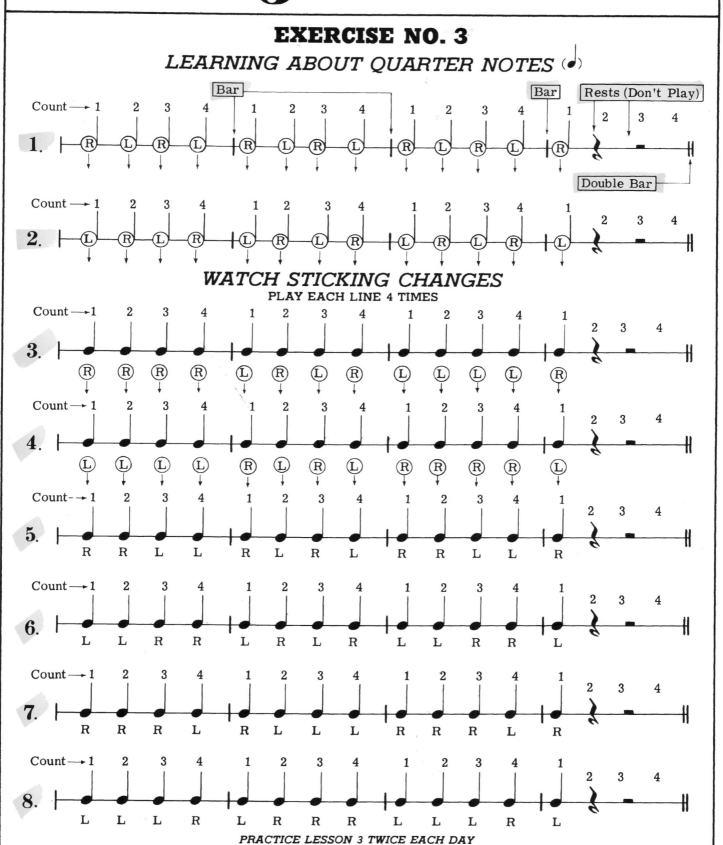

WATCH STICKING CHANGES
PLAY EACH LINE 4 TIMES

PRACTICE LESSON 3 TWICE EACH DAY

LET YOUR STICK BOUNCE.

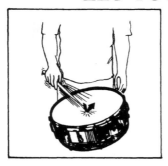

FIG. 23 The Right Hand Bounce

FIG. 24 The Left Hand Bounce

PRACTICE BOUNCING YOUR STICKS FOR SEVERAL MINUTES EACH DAY.
REPEAT 10 to 1 to 10 EXERCISE IN LESSON 1 USING BOUNCES.

Measure = Distance between Bar lines

EXERCISE NO. 4
RESTS—COUNT, BUT DON'T PLAY

Repeat to Beginning

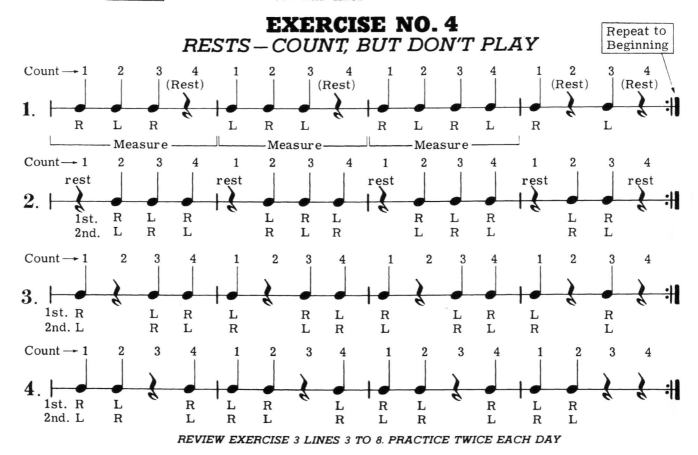

REVIEW EXERCISE 3 LINES 3 TO 8. PRACTICE TWICE EACH DAY

TIME (METER) SIGNATURES

$\frac{4}{4}$ $\frac{3}{4}$ $\frac{2}{4}$

$\frac{4}{4}$ = Top number tells how many counts in a measure.
Bottom numer tells what kind of a note gets one count.

Bottom Number Code

$\frac{1}{4}$ = Whole Note (o)   **2** = Half Note (♩)
$\frac{1}{4}$ = Quarter Note (♩)   **8** = Eighth Note (♪)

EXERCISE NO. 5

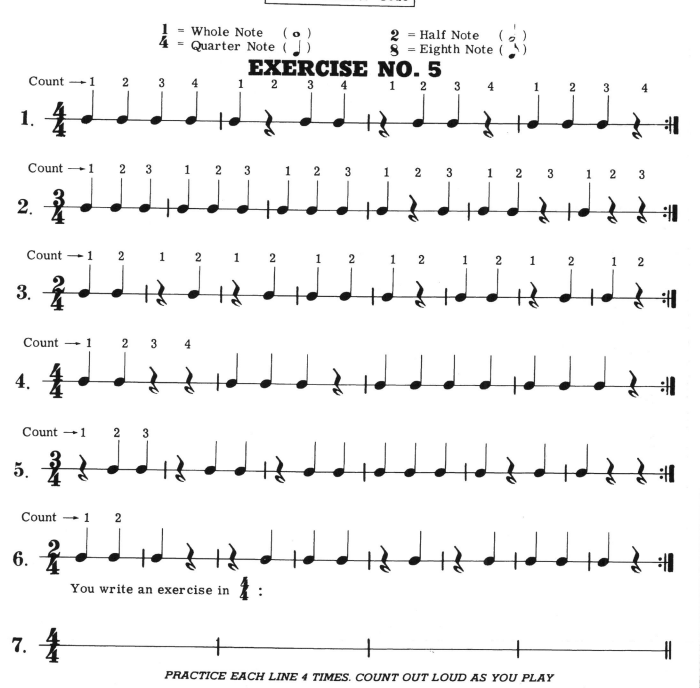

PRACTICE EACH LINE 4 TIMES. COUNT OUT LOUD AS YOU PLAY

EXERCISE NO. 6
CHANGE TIME AS YOU GO

EXERCISE NO. 7
BOUNCE ALONG

WHEN THE TIME SIGNATURES CHANGE, KEEP THE SPEED OF QUARTER NOTES THE SAME.

WHOLE AND HALF NOTES, THE TIE

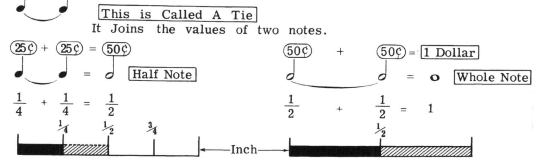

This is Called A Tie
It Joins the values of two notes.

(25¢) + (25¢) = (50¢)　　　　　　　(50¢) + (50¢) = 1 Dollar

= ♩ Half Note　　　　　　　= o Whole Note

$\frac{1}{4} + \frac{1}{4} = \frac{1}{2}$　　　　　　　$\frac{1}{2} + \frac{1}{2} = 1$

← Inch →

EXERCISE NO. 8

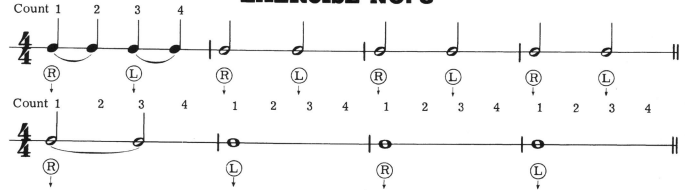

PUT THEM ALL TOGETHER

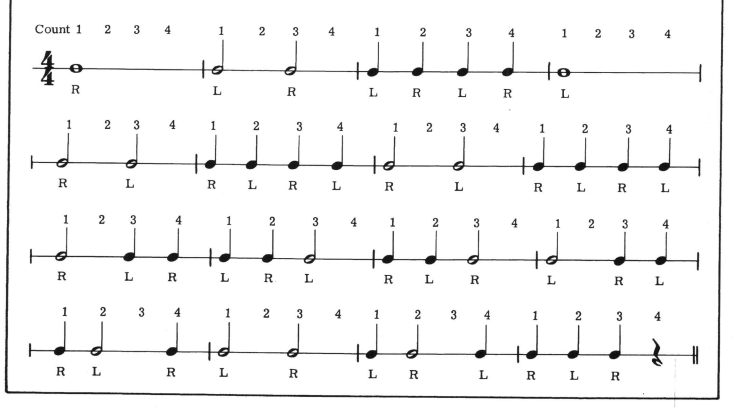

13

EXERCISE NO. 9
A DUET IS PLAYING TOGETHER WITH SOMEONE ELSE

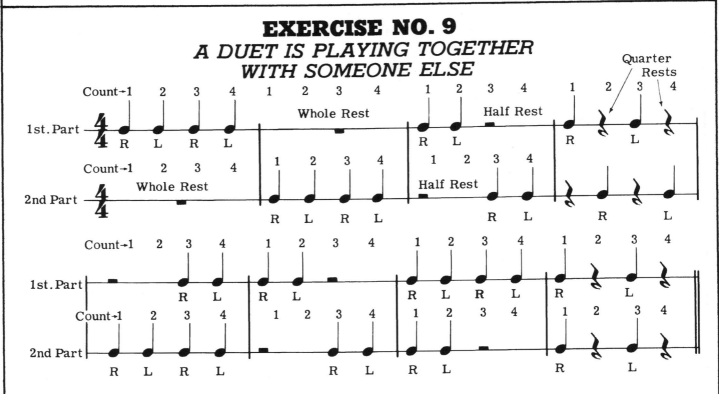

If you are in a class, divide the class in half. Have one half play part 1 and the other half play part 2.

If you have a recorder at home, record the 1st part, then play the 2nd part with the recorder. Count 1-2-3-4 before you start to play.

EXERCISE NO. 10
BOUNCES WITH HALF'S & QUARTER'S

STUDENT TEST #1

CIRCLE THE CORRECT ANSWER

1. ♩ IS CALLED A: HALF NOTE — QUARTER NOTE — REST

2.  |←————————→| BETWEEN THE BAR LINES IS CALLED:
REST — TIME SIGNATURE — MEASURE

3. 4/4 IS CALLED A: TIME SIGNATURE — MEASURE — REST

4.  ♪ IS A: HALF NOTE — BOUNCE BEAT — WHOLE NOTE

5. 𝅝 IS A: HALF NOTE — BOUNCE BEAT — WHOLE NOTE

6. ⁊ IS A: NOTE — BAR — REST

7. ♩♩ IS CALLED A: TIE — REST — BAR

8. ♩♩ = ♩ ♩ 𝅝

9. ♩♩ = ♩ ♩ 𝅝

10. 2/4 HOW MANY COUNTS IN A |MEASURE| ? 4 2 3

EXERCISE NO. 11
RESTS
OR HOW TO KEEP QUIET

PLAY SOME — REST SOME

EXERCISE NO. 12
REST TOGETHER
(DUET)

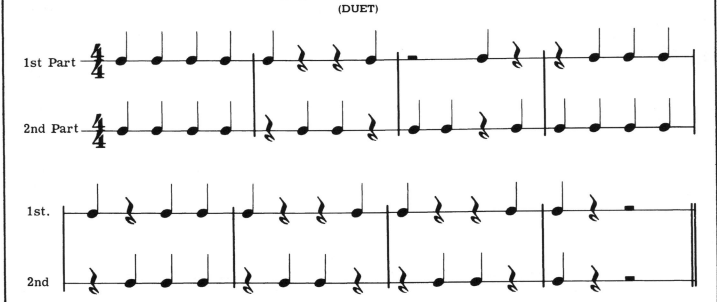

EXERCISE NO. 13
POGO STICK
BOUNCE & REST

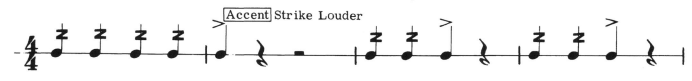

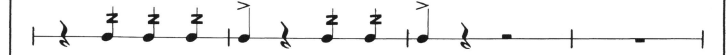

EXERCISE NO. 14
"MAGIC 16"
WITH BOUNCES

INTRODUCING 8TH NOTES

8th Notes are twice as fast as quarter Notes

(♪) single 8th Note   (♫) Two or more 8th notes are joined at the top.

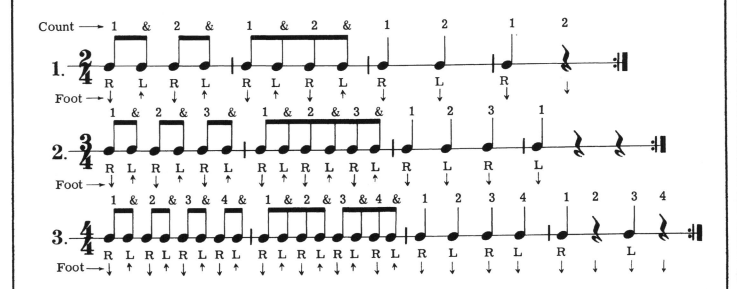

EXERCISE NO. 15
"MAGIC 16"
WITH 8TH NOTES

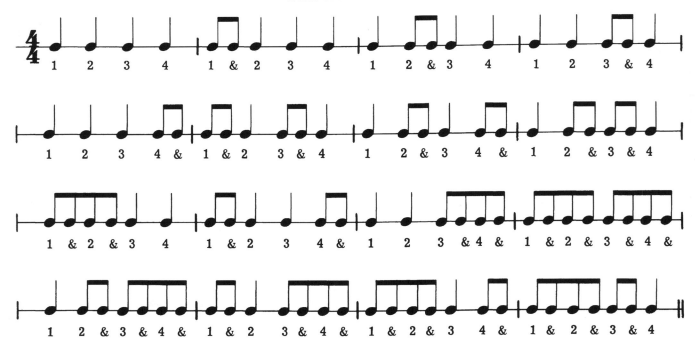

INTRODUCING 8TH RESTS

(**7**) 8th Rest equals the value of an 8th note (♪)

EXERCISE NO. 16
"MAGIC 16"
WITH 8TH RESTS

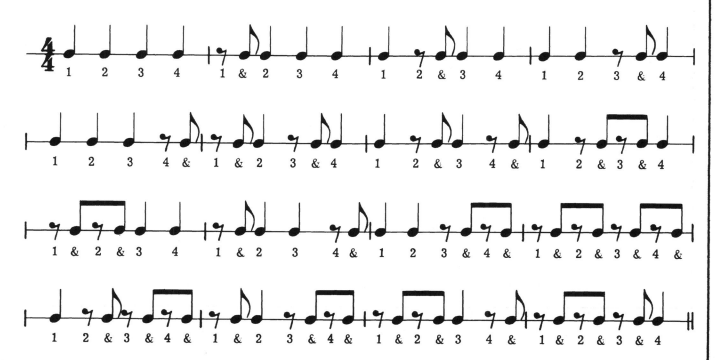

EXERCISE NO. 20
6/8 TIME

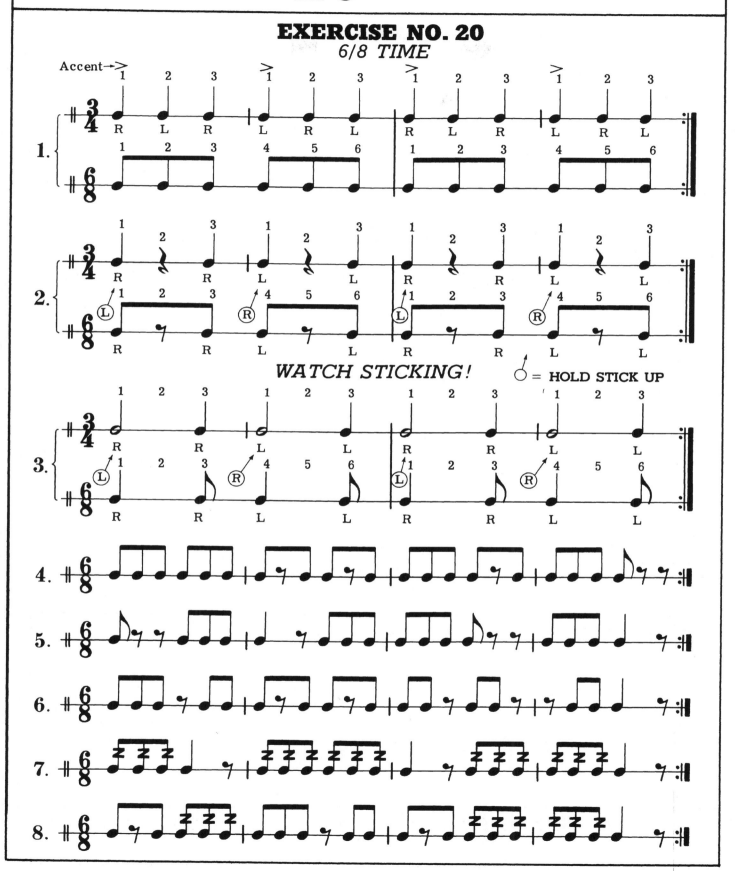

WATCH STICKING! ○ = HOLD STICK UP

EXERCISE NO. 21
REPEATS AND ENDINGS

Repeat   **Signs -** Play all of the music between these signs twice.   ⟋ = Repeat Measure

EXERCISE NO. 22
1ST & 2ND ENDINGS

Play through the 1st ending and Repeat.

The 2nd. time skip the 1st. Ending and play the 2nd. Ending.

LESSON 12

TEST YOUR SKILLS

1.

2.

3.

4.

5.

DYNAMICS CHART

Dynamic marks are the marks of expression in music.

THESE MARKS TELL YOU HOW LOUD OR SOFTLY YOU SHOULD PLAY

softest   *crescendo*   *loudest*   *decrescendo or diminuendo*   *softest*

ppp   *pp*   *p*   *mp*   *mf*   *f*   *ff*   *fff*   *ff*   *f*   *mf*   *mp*   *p*   *pp*   *ppp*

p = piano (soft)   *pp* = pianissimo (very soft)   *ppp* = pianissississimo (very, very soft)

f = forte (loud)   *ff* = fortissimo (very loud)   *fff* = fortississimo (very, very loud)

m = mezzo (moderate)   *mp* = mezzo piano (moderately soft)   *mf* = mezzo forte (moderately loud)

sfz = sfortzando [suddenly loud]

HOW TO USE A METRONOME

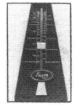

Keywound Type   Keywound Type Plastic   Electric   Elec. with flash

The metronome is used to find the correct speed (tempo) of a musical composition. Settings are from 40 to 208 beats per minute. For example ♩ = 120 would mean the speed of quarter notes was to be 120 beats per minute. These are listed at the beginning of a piece and where ever the speed changes.

A metronome can help you practice. Find the speed at which you can play a piece, then gradually increase the setting until you are able to reach the desired speed. If you mark the speed you can play a piece in the margin, you can always find the correct speed when you begin again. As you succeed in going faster, mark the new speed. Watch yourself improve.

REVIEW PIECE

= Bounce Beats

Contains only material in *A SNARE DRUM PRIMER*. Set your metronome to 76. Continue playing this piece until you can play it at 120 = ♩ .

♩ = 76 to 120

M.M. Speeds

— 76
— 80
— 84
— 88
— 92
— 96
—100
—104
—108
—112
—120

DYNAMIC MARKS are the signs which tell you how loud or soft to play. *f* stands for forte (loud). *p* stands for piano (soft).

CREATIVE WRITING NO. 1

Fill in the blank measures with a rhythm of your choice. Try several different rhythms until you find the one that sounds best, then write it in the blank space.

HOW TO UNDERSTAND THE TIME SIGNATURE

Top Number tells how many counts in each measure.
Bottom Number tells you the kind of note which gets 1 count.
Bottom Number Code: 1 = 𝅝   2 = 𝅗𝅥   4 = ♩   8 = ♪   16 = 𝅘𝅥𝅯
Thus: $\frac{3}{8}$ = 3 8th notes (♫) to a measure $\frac{2}{2}$ = 2 Half notes (𝅗𝅥 𝅗𝅥) to a measure
STUDY THE NOTE WHEELS IN LESSON 2

THE NOTE WHEELS

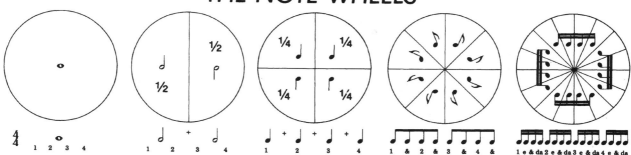

16TH NOTES

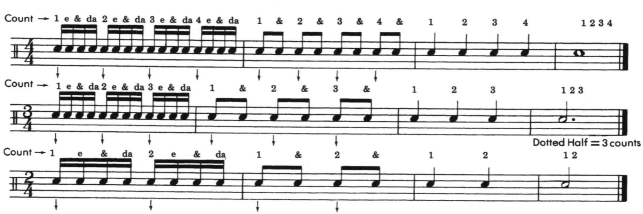

Dotted Half = 3 counts

COUNT AS YOU PLAY
"GROUP 16"

27

16TH NOTE RHYTHMS

4 16th Rests = 2 8th Rests = 1 Quarter Rest

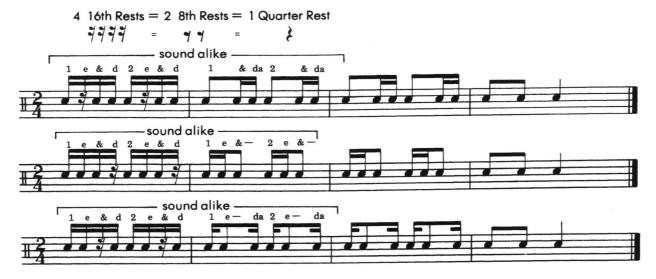

Play lines 1, 2, 3 several times each until you are sure you understand the rhythms.

MIX AND MATCH IN 2/4

mf = medium loud   *mp* = medium soft

LESSON 16

"DUET WITH 16TH NOTES"

sfz = sforzando = sudden strong accent.

CREATIVE WRITING NO. 2

Finish these exercises using one of the following note groups for each missing count.

1.

2.

3.

4.

5.

6.

> When you have finished writing, play each exercise to make sure it is the way you want it. Does it sound complete? Could you do it another way with better results? Experiment!

¢ ($\frac{2}{2}$) *CUT-TIME — ALLA BREVE*

In $\frac{2}{2}$ time a ♩ (Half note) equals 1 count, a 𝅝 (Whole note) equals 2 counts.

- COMPARISON CHART -

MIX AND MATCH IN ¢

"CUT-TIME DUET"

ff = very loud   **pp** = very soft

BOUNCES TO ROLLS

"ROLL ALONG"

¢ *CUT-TIME ROLLS*

"CUT-OFF MARCH"

★ *cresc* = *crescendo get louder gradually*

CREATIVE WRITING NO. 3

On the blank lines, write the exercise above using the correct roll notation. See example below.

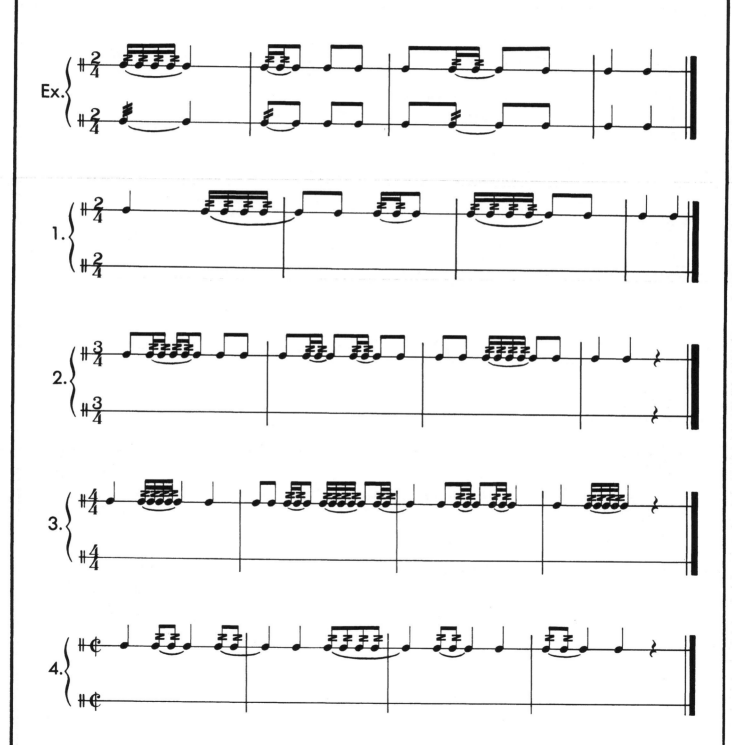

ROLL DUET #1

ROLL DUET #2

STUDENT TEST #2

17 - 20 EXCELLENT	SCORE
14 - 16 GOOD	
12 - 13 FAIR	
0 - 9 POOR	

1. How many counts do you give each of these notes in $\frac{4}{4}$ time?

o   ♩   ♩.   ♩

____   ____   ____   ____   **(4 points)**

2. Dynamic Marks: *ff*   *f*   *mf*   *mp*   *p*   *pp*

   Which mean: soft (   )   very loud (   )   medium loud (   )

              very soft (   )   loud (   )   medium soft (   )   **(6 points)**

3. Place the correct count under these rhythms.

(3 points)

4.   ▁▁▁▁▁◁   means to get _____

       ▷▔▔▔▔▔   means to get _____   **(2 points)**

5. Which rhythms sound the same?   Circle   your answer.

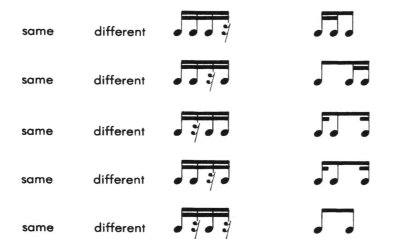

same   different

same   different

same   different

same   different

same   different   **(5 points)**

DOTTED NOTES AND THEIR VALUES

A dot after a note increases the value of the note by ½. Thus if a note equals 4 counts, the same note with a dot after it equals 4 plus (½) or 2 = 6 counts. Another way of thinking about dotted notes is that a dotted note equals 3 of the next smaller note. Thus a dotted whole note (o •) equals 3 half ( ) notes.

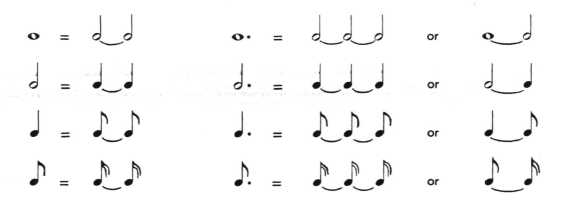

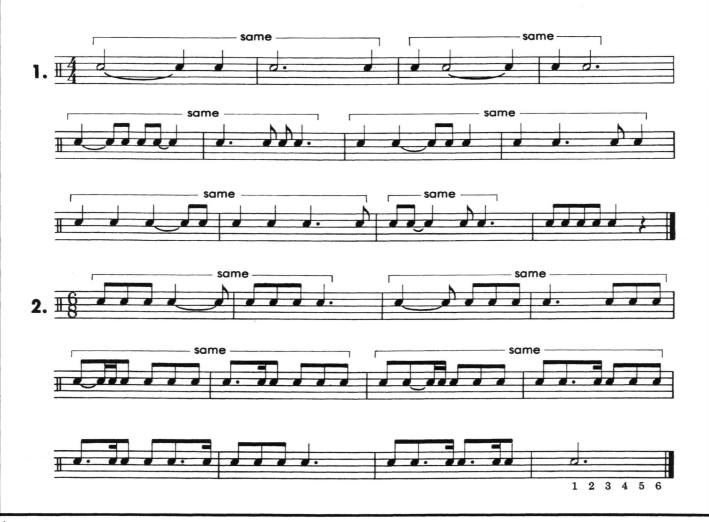

1 2 3 4 5 6

38

6/8 WITH 16TH NOTES

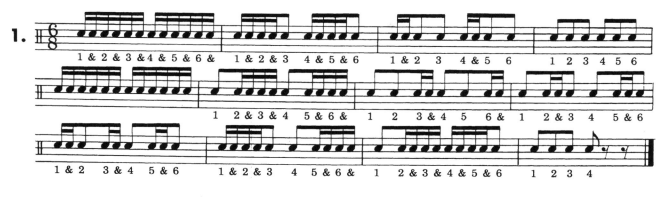

"TITLE 6"

"DO IT IN 6"

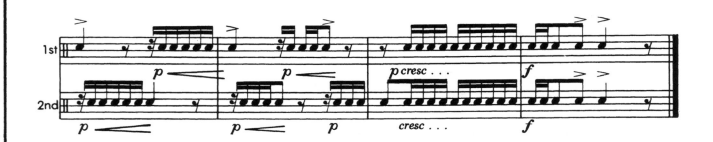

$\frac{6}{8}$ BOUNCES TO ROLLS

"SOLO SCENE"

"ROLL OVER AND DO IT AGAIN"

BASIC STICK STROKES

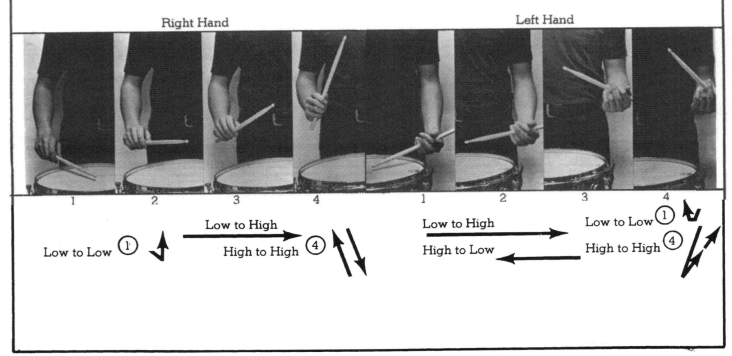

STUDENT TEST #3

MATCH THESE ROLLS WITH RHYTHMS ON THE RIGHT

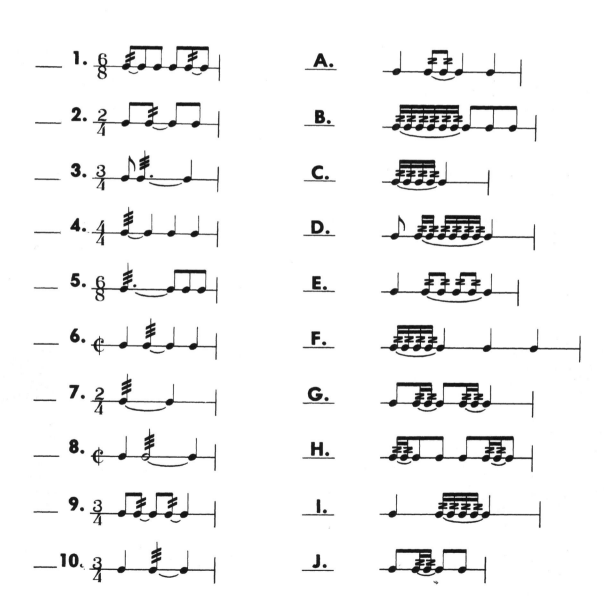

DIRECT FOLLOW THROUGH FLAMS

R. Flam   **L. Flam**

Starting with one hand high and one hand low, the high hand plays high to low and the low hand plays low to high. These movements are done at the same time. The result is a Direct Follow Through Flam. This is used for all alternate Flams.

Together in drumming this is called a flam.

Grace Note

REVERSE FOLLOW THROUGH FLAMS

R. Flam

L. Flam

Starting with one hand high and one hand low, the high hand plays high to high and the low hand plays low to low. These movements are done at the same time. The result is a Reverse Follow Through Flam. This is used for flams repeated in the same hand.

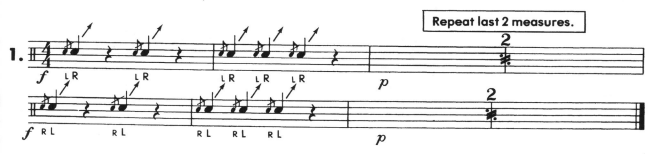

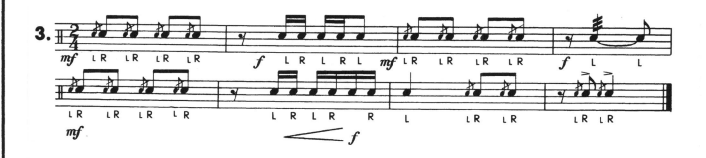

45

NO FOLLOW THROUGH FLAMS

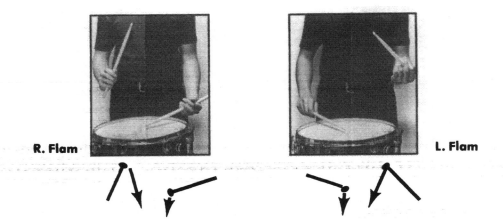

R. Flam   **L. Flam**

Starting with one hand high and one hand low, the high hand plays high to low and the low hand plays low to low. These movements are done at the same time. The result is a No Follow Through Flam. It is used whenever a flam is attached to a group of fast single notes.

STUDENT TEST #4

WHICH FLAM DO YOU USE?

DFT (Direct Follow Through)   **RFT** (Reverse Follow Through)   **NFT** *(No Follow Through)*

____ 1.

____ 2.

                     L R   R L   L R   R L

____ 3.

                     L R   L R   L R   L R

(CIRCLE) THE LOUDEST DYNAMIC MARK

4.   *p*   *f*

5.   *mf*   *ff*

6.   *mp*   *pp*

7.   *mf*   *p*

8.   Explain | 𝄽² |

9.   Draw a Crescendo

10.   Draw a Diminuendo

47

PURPLE FLAME DUET

FINAL PLAYING TEST

Teacher check off

FINAL WRITTEN TEST

17 - 20	EXCELLENT	SCORE
14 - 16	GOOD	
10 - 13	FAIR	
0 - 9	POOR	

USING ONE **NOTE**, COMPLETE EACH MEASURE.

1. $\frac{2}{4}$

2. $\frac{3}{4}$

3. $\frac{4}{4}$

4. $\frac{6}{8}$

5. $\mathcal{C}$

USING ONE **REST**, COMPLETE EACH MEASURE.

6. $\frac{4}{4}$

7. $\frac{6}{8}$

8. $\frac{2}{4}$

9. $\frac{3}{4}$

10. $\frac{2}{4}$

WRITE IN THE CORRECT DYNAMIC MARKS

11. Medium Loud _____

12. Very Loud _____

13. Very Soft _____

14. Loud _____

15. An Accent _____

16. Medium Soft _____

17. Get Louder _____

18. Soft _____

19. Get Softer _____

20. Sforzando _____

Certificate of Completion

This is to certify that

_____
STUDENT'S NAME

has now completed Mel Bay's Snare Drum Method. As a supplement to your level of advancement, I recommend Mel Bay's Fun with Drums.

_____
TEACHER'S NAME

_____
DATE

Made in the USA
San Bernardino, CA
10 October 2016